AN
EDWARDIAN
LADY'S
FLOWER
ALBUM

AN
EDWARDIAN
LADY'S
FLOWER
ALBUM

1913

FRANCES LINCOLN

For Jeanie
My mother
Aggie's grand-daughter
Who shared her love of flowers

Frances Lincoln Ltd
4 Torriano Mews
Torriano Avenue
London NW5 2RZ
www.franceslincoln.com

An Edwardian Lady's Flower Album
Copyright © Frances Lincoln Ltd 2005
Text and illustrations copyright ©
Mary Clare Cornwallis

The publishers would like to thank
A.P. Watt Ltd on behalf of Michael B. Yeats
for permission to reproduce an extract from
The Land of Heart's Desire by W.B. Yeats.

A catalogue record for this book is available from
The British Library

ISBN 0 7112 2528 1

Printed in Singapore

First Frances Lincoln edition 2005

9 8 7 6 5 4 3 2 1

AGNES KATHERINE LANDALE

What we as children called the 'Treasure Room' stood at the top of the stairs in my maternal grandparents' house in Kent. We were only allowed to enter this haven on rare occasions, and even then only if were were accompanied by an adult, but my memories of it are as clear today as they were when my grandmother died in 1965.

It was full of all manner of things – such as beads, ostrich feather fans, Ascot hats and leather spats – objects to fascinate and entrance us children, but among the many books and folders, which recorded the lives of two prosperous Edwardian families, was a large green box containing this special treasure you are holding today. Its pages, full of vibrant colour and well-chosen verses, were beautifully bound in green leather with gold lettering stating simply: 'Flower Calendar 1913 A.K. Landale'.

Agnes Katherine Landale, or Aggie as she was known to her family and friends, was born in Liverpool in 1851, the only daughter of George Henderson, a Scottish merchant who specialized in Indian Jute. Her grandfather, John Henderson, had moved from Borrowstounness to Glasgow at the turn of the century and, with his brother

HEVERSWOOD HOUSE, AGNES' CHILDHOOD HOME

TWO OF HER BROTHERS

Robert, had established the firm of R. & J. Henderson, which 'by dint of patient toil, prudent forethought and wise economy', had become one of the most successful trading firms in that city. When he died childless in 1867 he left his huge fortune to be divided between his nieces and nephews, who included Aggie's father.

In fact, most of her relatives were merchants or traders with India and she grew up at Heverswood, a large house, now demolished, in Brasted in the Weald of Kent. She had three brothers to whom she always remained close and she appears to have had a happy childhood. She was particularly devoted to her sister-in-law Laura Henderson, an amazing woman whose life has supplied the storyline for two films, the latest starring Dame Judi Dench. Aggie married David Guild Landale, another Indian merchant with a Scottish background (and ten brothers and sisters), on April 30, 1879. She went to Paris to buy the wedding dresses for herself and her bridesmaids.

The Landales at that time owned one tenth of the jute looms in Bengal. David's most famous relative had been another David Landale, a Kirkcaldy merchant who, in 1826, successfully fought the last recorded duel in Scotland after a disagreement with his bank manager. His opponent, George Morgan, 'an arrogant and unpopular man', had secretly practised his shooting before the duel; Landale, who had never fired a shot in his life, simply put his trust in his God. While the bank manager missed, Landale's shot mortally wounded the other man. How many of us today must wish we could deal with financial advisers in the same way!

At the subsequent court proceedings in Perth, the jury found Landale not guilty of murder without even retiring and he left the court with his character still honourable and unsullied. At the same session the judge Lord Gillies sentenced a twelve-year-old girl to transportation for seven years for stealing eight shillings. Robert Leekie, who pleaded guilty to stealing some silver 'in consequence of want', was sentenced to be executed. Another prisoner, sentenced to fourteen years' transportation for stealing from a bleaching green, observed that there was plenty of law that day but damned little justice. Strangely enough, within thirty years the same Landale and Morgan families were united

HER HUSBAND, DAVID GUILD LANDALE, AND FIRST SON, RUSSELL

by marriage and founded an Indian mercantile firm in their joint names.

David and Aggie had four children of their own. She clearly shared her husband's work and travels, as two of their children were born in India and another in Monte Carlo. A recently discovered letter written from Calcutta in 1880 describes her happy and comfortable life in India with David and her oldest son, Russell, who was my grandfather. The letter, written to her sister-in-law

Isabelle, starts 'Dearest old girl,' and continues

Many thanks for your letter last mail and the enclosure about Mr Jenkin's marriage – so he has married one of those fast Tolers! Evidently she must be very pretty from what they say but what an odd idea to live with his mama-in-law – not very nice I should fancy. . . . And fancy Ernest Secretan engaged! I was amazed – how could a nice girl be so idiotic as to take him – however tastes differ.

After living in India, Aggie and David eventually settled in The Grange, a large and unattractive red-brick building in the pretty Surrey village of Limpsfield. The house is still standing, with the initials DGL visible over the drawing room window, but it is now a school for children with special educational needs. The National Census of 1891 records that apart from the family of six there were twelve live-in staff at the house.

The garden was tended by an additional team of eight, who mainly lived above the stables. It was this garden that in 1913 gave Aggie the inspiration for her Flower Calendar. It was extremely large, with far-reaching views down to a lake and the village church beyond. It must have had an abundance of colour, as it overflowed with plants of all shapes and sizes some brought back from the family's travels abroad. An enormous greenhouse ran the full length of the walled garden and was crammed with peaches, nectarines and grapes. Although the house and garden have seen many changes, there is still some evidence of the formal layout which was so fashionable at the time.

I have always assumed that she worked so assiduously on her calendar to overcome the grief of losing her husband the previous year, after thirty-three years together. I do not know what artistic training she had but, in my opinion, the calendar is almost perfect in its layout. Apart from the skill and observation involved in the painting, she also appears to have been extremely well-read and her choice of verse is original and refreshing. To add to her talents she was also an exceptionally able needlewoman.

She was not to know the full horrors about to be unleashed the following year with the start of the Great War. She lost her adored nephew Alexander Henderson, Laura's only child, shot by a German sniper in 1915 and died herself the following year at the age of sixty-three.

Her two daughters clearly inherited her talent and exhibited their watercolours in Bond Street in 1911. My grandfather, Russell Landale, married Gladys Phipps in 1919 and it was she who was the guardian of the Treasure Room of my childhood.

The Phipps of Chalcot in Wiltshire had made their fortunes importing coffee and bananas from South America, particularly Brazil, just as the Hendersons and Landales had made their fortunes with jute from the East. Bizarrely enough a Phipps of Chalcot had fought a duel with a neighbour over a poaching dispute two years before the Landale duel.

Gladys's first fiancé, Geoff Kiddle, an Australian rancher, had died serving with the British Forces in what is now Iraq in 1917 and unbelievably she went out there on her own to visit his grave that same year. She kept all the letters he sent her from Iraq and from his first tour of duty in the trenches on the Western Front, written in pencil in a hurried, scrawled and almost indecipherable hand. She also kept every letter from my grandfather in India, written at the same time, in which he expressed the same love and devotion to her as Kiddle.

In fact she kept everything. So in the Treasure Room there were mementos

WATERCOLOUR FROM AGNES' SKETCHBOOK

of Kiddles, Hendersons, Landales and Phipps, of the royal princes of Siam (who seemed to be regular correspondents and visitors to Chalcot), of her brother Charles (who married the daughter of the Duke of Buccleuch and was thus related in marriage to our own Royal Family), of her eldest sister's family when her husband Sir John Fuller had been Governor of Victoria, and of Dame Nellie Melba, to whom she had once been a companion. Here, too, was the Flower Calendar of Agnes Katherine Landale.

Aggie was buried in Limpsfield churchyard next to her husband. Surprisingly there is no headstone for them but near by are buried Frederick Delius, Sir Thomas Beecham, Percy Grainger and Eileen Joyce, all of whom contributed to the artistic heritage of Britain and it would be nice to think that the Flower Calendar of A.K. Landale could also make a contribution in its own small way.

The poem below in Aggie's handwriting slipped out of the calendar only recently. Perhaps Aggie could not find a place for it, or perhaps it was meant to be at the beginning.

Mary Clare Cornwallis

Flowers of the cheerful days of Spring
Come at my magic summoning!
Flowers of the Summer's golden age
Come when I call to deck my page!
Bright things that, as the year grows old,
Light the sad Earth with red and gold,
And flowers that bloom in Winter snows,
Sweet snowdrops, or a Christmas rose:-
Come at my touch, that all who look
May see you mirrored in my book.

Anon.

January

1

Winter Aconite

Silver & gold! The Snowdrop white
And yellow blossomed Aconite,
Waking from winters slumber cold,
Their hoarded treasures now unfold,
And scatter them to left & right.
R. Wilton

2

Seeds of
Sycamore

3

Each is commission'd, could we trace
The voyage to each decreed,
To convoy to some distant place
A pilgrim seed;

Xmas Rose

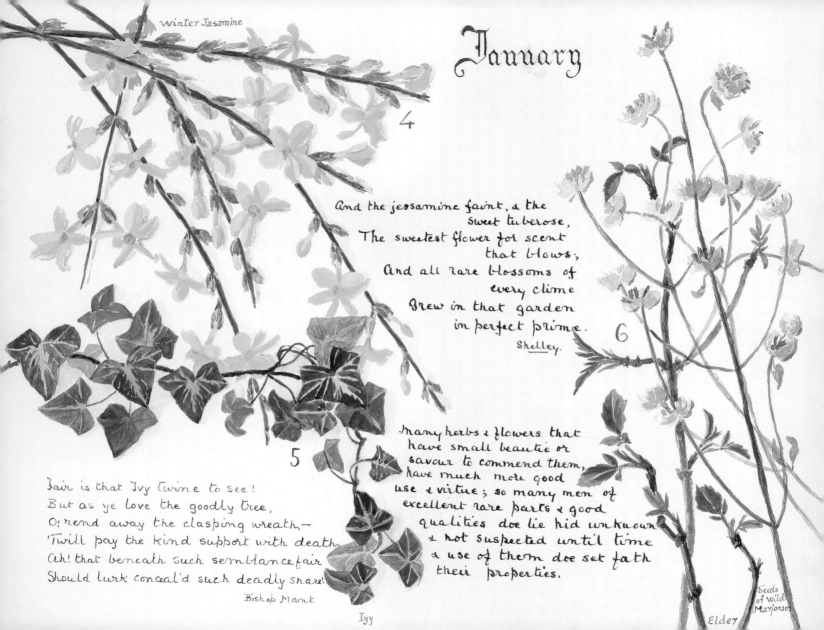

January

Winter Jasamine

4

And the jessamine faint, & the
Sweet tuberose,
The sweetest flower for scent
that blows;
And all rare blossoms of
every clime
Grew in that garden
in perfect prime.
Shelley.

6

5

Fair is that Ivy twine to see!
But as ye love the goodly tree,
O! rend away the clasping wreath,—
'Twill pay the kind support with death.
Ah! that beneath such semblance fair
Should lurk conceal'd such deadly snare!
Bishop Mant

Many herbs & flowers that
have small beautie or
savour to commend them,
have much more good
use & virtue; so many men of
excellent rare parts & good
qualities doe lie hid unknown
& not suspected until time
& use of them doe set fath
their properties.

Ivy

Seeds
of Wild
Marjoram

Elder

January

Cold as the wind of early Spring,
Chilling the buds that still lie sheathed
In their brown armour with its sting.
And the bare branches withering —
— — — — — — — — — — — — — — —
Cold as the March wind's bitterness.

7

9

The woodland willow
  stands a lonely bush
Of nebulous gold
Where the Spring-goddess
  cowers in faint-
    attire
Of frightened fire

Robert Bridges

8

The merest grass along the roadside
              as we pass
  Lichen & moss & sturdy weed
Tell of His love who sends the dew
The rain and sunshine too
To nourish one small seed! C. Rossetti.

Seeds of
wild Sage

Palm

Dog-Mercury

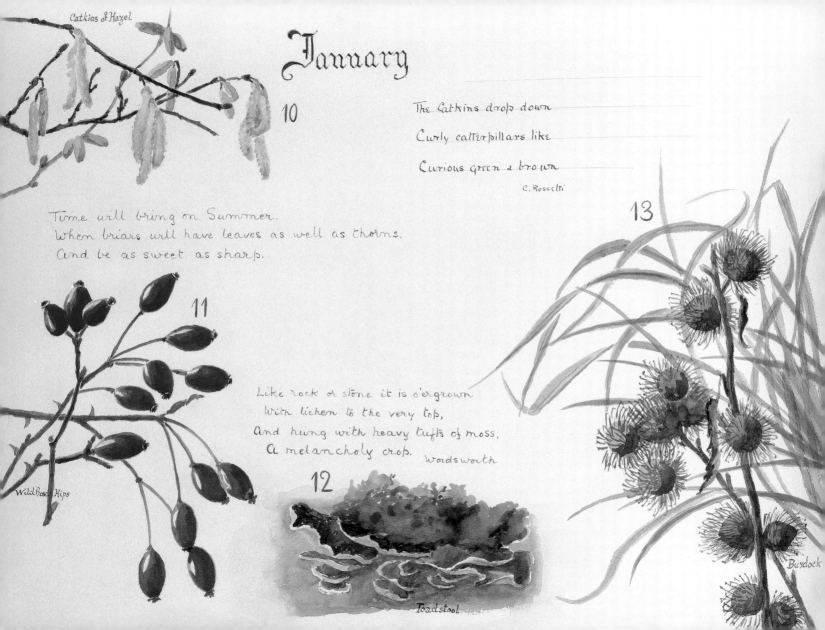

Catkins of Hazel

January

10

The Catkins drop down
Curly catterpillars like
Curious green & brown
C. Rossetti

Time will bring on Summer,
When briars will have leaves as well as thorns,
And be as sweet as sharp.

11

13

Like rock or stone it is o'ergrown
With lichen to the very top,
And hung with heavy tufts of moss,
A melancholy crop.   Wordsworth

12

Wild Rose Hips

Toadstool

Burdock

Seeds of
Wild Clematis

14

Like an oaken stock in winter woods

O'erflourished with the hoary clematis

Tennyson

15

If Janiveer calends be summerly gay,
'Twill be winterly weather till the calends of May

16

Oak-apple

Mahonia

Beech Masts

January

.... the bare Earth, till then

17

Desert & bare, unsightly, unadorn'd,

Brought forth the tender grass, whose verdure clad

Her universal face with pleasant green:

Then herbs of every leaf, that sudden flower'd,

Opening their various colours, and made gay

Her bosom, smelling sweet:

Milton

Life is a folded flower, & what it holds
We know not, till unfolding leaf by leaf,
It shews God's secret hidden in its folds,
And bares its fragrant heart to vision brief.

18

19

Tiarella cordifolia

Laurel
Daphne

January

Groundsel

20

Each is commission'd, could we trace
The voyage to each decreed,
To convoy to some distant place
A pilgrim seed.

21

Seeds of
Fleabane

23

Snowdrop

22

24

It is the herald of the flowers,
Sent with its small white flag of truce, to plead
For its beleaguer'd brethren: suppliantly
It prays stern Winter to withdraw his troop
Of winds & blustering storms, & having won
A smile of promise from its pitying foe,
Returns to tell the issue of its errand
To the expectant host.

Westwood

Seeds of
St John's Wort

Seeds of
Yarrow

26

25

Dead
nettle

Double
snowdrop

Chickweed

27

Lenten rose

29

Giant
snowdrop

28

You ask why Spring's fair first-born flower is white:
Peering from out the warm earth long ago,
It saw above its head great drifts of snow,
And blanched with fright!

Scollard

Brothers, joy to you! I've brought some
        snowdrops

Just a few.
But quite enough to prove the worlds awake
Cheerful and hopeful in the frosty dew,
And for the pale sun's sake

Chr: Rossetti

Gorgeous flowerets in the Sunlight shining
  Blossoms flaunting in the eye of day,
Tremulous leaves, with soft & silver lining,
  Buds that open only to decay;

January

Not alone in Spring's armorial bearing,
  And in Summer's green-emblazoned field,
But in arms of brave old Autumn's wearing,
  In the centre of his brazen shield;

Everywhere about us are they glowing,
  Some like stars to tell us Spring is born;
Others, their blue eyes with tears o'erflowing,
  Stand like Ruth amid the golden corn;

Not alone in meadows & green valleys,
  On the mountain top, & by the brink
Of sequestered pools in woodland alleys
  Where the slaves of nature stoop to drink;

In all places then, & in all seasons
  Flowers expand their light & soul-like wings,
Teaching us by most persuasive reasons,
  How akin they are to human things.

30

Blue
hepatica

Up among the mountains,
In soft and mossy cell
By the silent springs and fountains
The lovely wild-flowers grow

31

Sax. oppositifolia

Blue.tit

February

Sax. sancta

1

Crocus

3

2

4

And the Spring arose on the garden fair
Like the Spirit of Love felt everywhere
And each flower & herb on Earth's
dark breast
Rose from the dreams of its
wintry rest.

Seeds of Euonymus

February

Pyrus japonica

5

6
Crocus

And at their feet the crocus brake like fire
Tennyson

Thro' lush green grasses burned the red anemone
Tennyson

7

8

Anemone
fulgens

Spring
Snowflake

When the Snowdrop goes to town
In her little grandmotherly bonnet,
With only a glamour of earth
And a magic of heaven upon it,
Look at the rainbow of Spring
In the eyes of the happy beholders!
Cares in a covey take wing,
And weariness falls from the shoulders.

Norman Gale

February

Prunus Pissardi

I have in my heart a vision of

spring begun

In sheltering wood, that feels the

kiss of the sun.

R. Bridges

10

11

Freesia

9

Now in the dark of february rains
Poor lovers of the sunshine,
Spring is born,
The earthy fields are full of
hidden corn,
And march's violets bud along
the lanes
G. Macdonald

Daphne
mezereum

February

Almond

12

mark well the flowering Almond in the wood;
If odorous blooms the bearing branches load,
The glebe will answer to the sylvan reign,
Great heats will follow, & large crops of grain
But if a wood of leaves o'ershade the tree
Such, and so barren will the
harvest be.

13

Alder

To win the secret
of a weed's
14 plain heart. Shepherds
purse

15

Spurge

February

Triteleia

16

Prunus triloba

17

18

Sax. Burseriana

And with child-like credulous affection,
We behold their tender buds expand;
Emblems of our own great resurrection,
Emblems of the bright & better land
                        Longfellow.

Fair Primrose haunts the shadow

With children of the Spring
                        R. Bridges

19

..... Primroses to fling
Before the door to make a golden path
For them to bring good luck into
        the house.
                        Yeats

Primrose

February

Rhododendron praecox

20

Andromeda floribunda

21

Forsythia

22

Celandine

23

The Celandine,
The starry herald of that gentlest gale,
Whose plumes are sunbeams dipped
in odours fine.

Pansies, lilies, kingcups, daisies,
Let them live upon their praises
Long, as there's a sun that sets,
Primroses will have their glory;
Long as there are violets,
They will have a place in story;
There's a flower that shall be mine
'Tis the little celandine.
Wordsworth

February

Pheasantseye

24

Time remembered is grief forgotten,
And frosts are slain & flowers begotten
And in green underwood & cover
Blossom by blossom the Spring begins.

The slim crocus stirs the winter snow

25

Crocus

26

Anémone
pulsatilla

February

27

Kerria

28

Chionodoxa
Luciliae

The same sweet violets bloom again;
The same blue skies and soft clean rain;
The birds their song once more renew;
Is it the Spring last year we knew?
This year Spring comes with fairer face,
To lend the garden sweeter grace.
But oh! how dearer than the past
Is this new Spring come back at last!

March

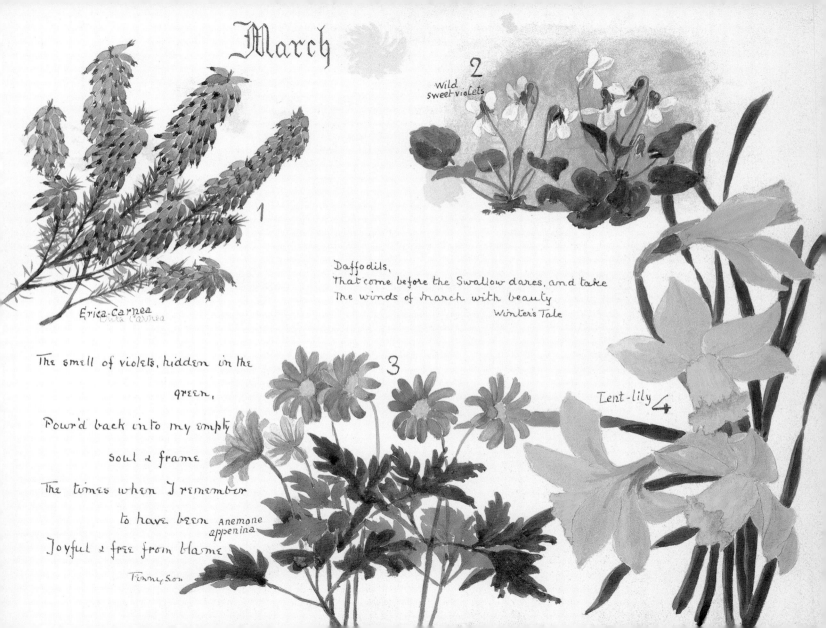

1 Erica carnea

2 Wild sweet violets

Daffodils,
That come before the Swallow dares, and take
The winds of March with beauty
     Winter's Tale

The smell of violets, hidden in the
    green,
Pour'd back into my empty
    soul & frame
The times when I remember
    to have been
Joyful & free from blame
    Tennyson

3 Anemone appenina

4 Tent-lily

March

When Spring unlocks the
flowers
To paint the laughing soil
Heber

Violet

5

Violet is for faithfulness,
Which in me shall abide
Hoping, likewise, that from your heart
You will not let it slide.

Pulmonaria

6

The verdant earth,

Like beauty awaking from a happy dream,

Lies smiling.......

Who passes down the wintry street?
7
Hey, ho, daffodil!
A sudden flame of
gold & sweet,
With sword
of emerald
girt so meet
And golden
gay from head to feet.

- - - - - - -
double Lent lily King trumpeter to Flora queen
Hey, ho, daffodil!
Blow, & the golden jousts begin
K.T. Hinkson

Chionodoxa

8

March

9

wood
Anemone

The windflower chilly
With all the winds at play

Cuckoo-flower

10

And by the meadow trenches blow
the faint sweet cuckoo flower
Tennyson.

11

Butter
&
Eggs

12

ground
Ivy

March

While yet we wait for Spring, & from the dry
And blackening east that so embitters march,
13 Well housed must watch grey fields & meadows parch,
And driven dust & withering snowflake flys;
Already in glimpses of the tarnish'd sky
The sun is warm & beckons to the larch,
And where the covert   hazels interarch
Their tassell'd twigs,   fair buds of primrose lie

Beneath the crisp &
wintry carpet hid
A million buds but stay their blossoming;
And trustful birds have built their nests amid
The shuddering boughs, & only wait to sing
Till one soft shower from the south shall bid,
And hither tempt the pilgrim steps of Spring

Epimedium

14

Adoxa
Moschtell

15

Berberis Darwinii

16

Polyanthus

R. Bridges

March

Ribes

17

...... the narcissi, the fairest among them all

Who gaze on their eyes in the streams recess

Till they die of their own dear loveliness

Shelley.

18

19

small-periwinkle

Stella

Thro' primrose tufts in that sweet bower

The periwinkle trail'd its wreaths;

And 'tis my faith, that every

flower

Enjoys the air it breathes

Wordsworth

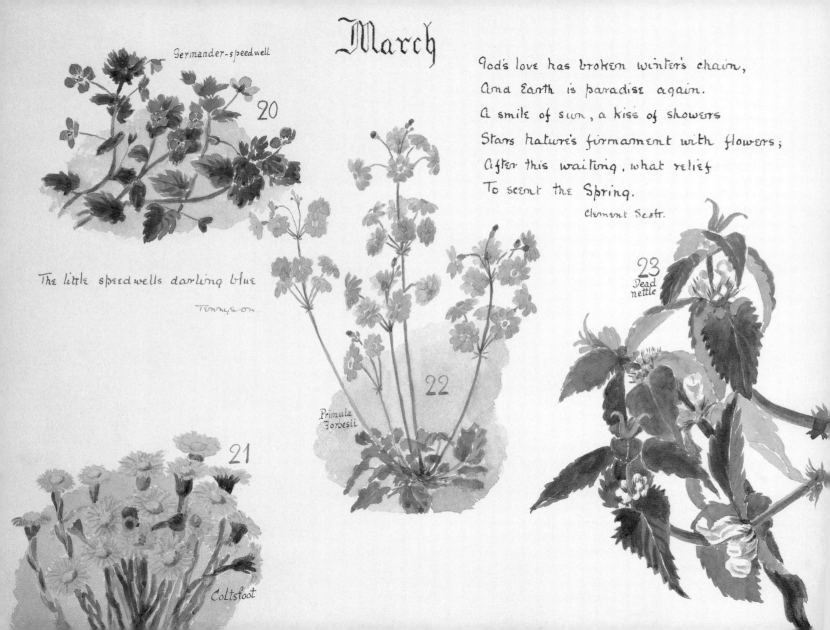

March

Germander-speedwell

20

The little speedwells darling blue

Tennyson.

God's love has broken winter's chain,
And Earth is paradise again.
A smile of sun, a kiss of showers
Stars nature's firmament with flowers;
After this waiting, what relief
To scent the Spring.

Clement Scott.

21

Coltsfoot

22

Primula Forbesii

23
Dead nettle

March

Primula farinosa

24

hepatica

25

When the hounds of Spring are on Winter's trace,
The mother of months in meadow or plain
Fills the shadows and windy places
With lisp of leaves and ripple of rain.

Swinburne

26

27

..... those bright wilding blooms
Won by the mountain climber. Theirs
the forms
And tints the most delightsome,
theirs the charm
The aureole flung along the silent heights
Whereon they frolic, children of the dew
And dancing waters

Golden saxifrage

Primula rosea

T.M. Coan

March

Old Earth is a pleasure to see
In sunshiny cloak of red and green;
The furrow lies fresh; this year will be
As years that are past have been.

Carlyle

28
Grape
hyacinth

29
Primula
denticulata

Soon shall the pied wind flowers
Babble of greening hours,
Primrose and daffodil
Yearn to the fathering sun
The lark have all his will,
The thrush be never done.
And April, May and June
Go to the same blithe tune
As this blithe dream of mine

W.E. Henley

30
Asarum
europaeum

31

April

And dreaming, some of autumn
past,
And some of spring approaching
fast,
And some of April buds
and showers,
And some of songs
in July bowers,
And all of love
Shelley

Dog-tooth
violet

The furzy prickles fire the dells
Tennyson

Prickly furze buds lavish gold
Keats

In the red April dawn,
In the wild April weather,
From brake, and thicket and lawn
The birds sung altogether.

Of a world still young—
still young!
Whose last word won't be said,
nor her last song dreamed
and sung,
Till her last true lovers dead!
W. E. Henley

Blackthorn

2

3

Gorse

April

Wild-sorrel

4

These skies are blue,
    Albeit they are seen
Both overhead & through
The bare boughs' open screen;
    Bare boughs that are not dead,
    But softly overspread
    With buds a little red,
    And vivid mists of green.

Their shadows fall,
    With clear-cut line on line,
Across green mosses all
    Starr'd with the celandine,
    Until their intricate
    Dark meshes seem a net
    Cast on a beach where wet
And lustrous agates shine.

5

Let April be
    Enthronëd on the hills
    With ancient dignity
While her birds' music thrills
    All heaven, & the ways
    That lead up to her daïs
    Are golden with the blaze
Of her own daffodils.

6

Sir Watkin

Lords & Lady
or
Jack in the pulpit
or
Cuckoo pint

April

A gold and silver cup
Upon a pillow green
Earth holds her daisy up
To catch the sunshine in

Sutton.

7

Daisy

8

O blooming white Narcissus. bud that lendest
New beauty to the meadow where
thou bendest!
The Spring without thy scent were nought,
Scarce worth one thought

J. A. Symonds

N. poeticus

Dear common flower. that grow'st
beside the way
fringing the dusty road
with harmless gold.

Lowel.

Dandelions to tell the hours
That never are told again

Housman

Dandelion

April

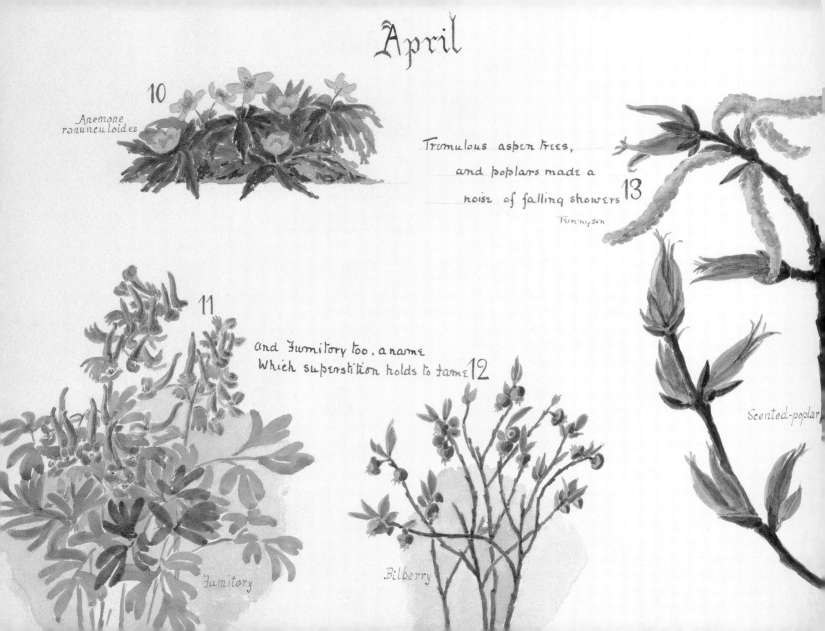

10

Anemone
ranunculoides

Tremulous aspen trees,
    and poplars made a
    noise of falling showers
        Tennyson
13

11

And Fumitory too, a name
Which superstition holds to tame 12

Fumitory

Bilberry

Scented-poplar

April

14 Dog-violet

Smell of my Violets! I found
        them where
The liquid south stole o'er them,
        on a bank
That leaned to running water.
        There's to me
A daintiness about these early flowers
That touches me like poetry.

15

frail wind flowers quake
        C. Rossetti

Anemone
Robinsoniana

16

Wallflower

April

Sound of vernal showers
    On the twinkling grass,
    Rain awaken'd flowers
    All that ever was
Joyous, and clear, and fresh......
                    Shelley

The marigold that goes to bed with the sun,
And with him rises weeping.

17

18

Aubretia

Fritillaria

19

Marsh
marigold

April

Cottage-Maid

20

How like a little child April appears:
Now sad & downcast, weeping o'er some ill;
Then, on a sudden, sobbing, sighing still,
Lifting her face, & laughing through her tears
L. M. A.

22

21

Viola gracilis

And the hyacinth, purple & white
& blue
Which flung from its bells a
sweet peal anew
Of music so delicate soft & intense, Wild
hyacinth
It was felt like an odour
within the sense.
Shelley

April

23

Loveliest of trees the cherry now
Is hung with bloom along the bough
And stands about the woodland side
Wearing white for Eastertide.

a. Housman

double
cherry

By rivulet or spring or wet roadside

That blue & bright eyed flow'ret

of the brook

Hope's gentle gem the sweet

24

25

forget me no

St Brigid
anemone

Wild
forget-me-not

April

Then laugheth the year; with flowers the meads are bright;

The bursting branches are tipped with flames of light;

The landscape is light; the dark clouds flee above,

And the shades of the land are a blue that is deep

as love.

R. Bridges

Corydalis
cheilanthifolius

26

In their gold coats spots you see

Those be rubies, fairy favours

In those freckles live their savours

Shakespeare

27

Cowslip

Yet shall the blue-eyed gentian look

Through fringed lids to Heaven

28

Gentian
acaulis

April

April, April,
Laugh thy girlish laughter,
Then, the moment after
Weep thy girlish tears!
April, that mine ears
Like a lover greetest,
If I tell thee sweetest,
All my hopes and fears;
April, April,
Laugh thy golden laughter
But the moment after,
Weep thy golden tears

29

Dalibardia

Genista
praecox

30

Is this a time to be cloudy
and sad,
When our mother nature laughs
around?
When even the deep blue heavens
look glad,
And gladness breathes from
the blossoming ground
Bryant.

May

Come into the garden. The wind blows
sharply from the north where the snow still lies,
& the clouds hang low, yet it

1 is May-day.

Larch

2

When rosy plumelets
tuft the larch.

Tennyson

3

She will bring thee, all together,
All delights of summer-weather;
All the buds & bells of May
From dewy sward or thorny spray

Keats

Single-tulips

Welsh
poppy

May

5

Heuchera
sanguinea

4

Ranunculus
acris

A bush of Mayflowers with the bees about them,
Ah! sure no tasteful nook would be without them!
And let a lush laburnum oversweep them,
And let long grass grow round the roots to keep them
Moist, cool & green; and shade the Violets
That they may bind the moss in leafy nets

Keats

7

6
Sax.
Guildford-seedling

violas
violas

May

Prunus triloba fl.pl

8

A single cloud on a sunny day,
While all the rest of heaven is clear,
A frown upon the atmosphere,
That hath no business to appear
When skies are blue & earth is gay
Byron

Cheiranthus
Marshalli
9

Lily-of-the-Valley
& seed

10

.... with her trembling
banner of perfum'd bells
The Lily of th valley & the jasmine,
Princesses twain in maiden fragrance
sure.
T.M. Coan

May

wild-Crab-apple

Beneath the Apple blossom in the Spring
When the pink cascades are falling

The flowers lift their faces
  With tears and smiles, after rain;
And all their pent-up sweetness
  Bursts forth, unchecked, again.
And the garden is filled with fragrance,
  Like the house where Mary shed
Her precious ointment of spikenard
  Over the Saviour's head
                              E. Read

11

12

Bugle

13

Auricula

May

Adder's tongue

15

14

Campion

God made the flowers to beautify
The earth, & cheer man's careful mood;
And he is happiest who hath power
To gather wisdom from a flower,
And wake his heart in every hour
To pleasant gratitude.

Wordsworth.

16

Choysia ternata

May

P. malus atrosanguinea

17

18

Archangel

19

Early-purple
Orchis

May

O! lovely flowers, my ever faithful friends!
Ye are the sweetest poetry of earth;
Ye are the dim forshadowings of heaven.

P. de Montgomery.

Herb-Robert

20

'Tis like the birthday of the world,

When Earth was born in bloom;

The light is made of many dyes

The air is all perfume

Tom Hood

21

Scilla
campanulata

22

Mountain Avens

May

23 Solomon's Seal

Ivory pendants in ordered rows
Hanging where jade green
　　　　leaves reveal
The sheen which the sunshine's
　　　　love bestows
　　Solomon's Seal,
　　　Solomon's Seal!

25

24

Deep tulips,

dash'd with fiery dew
Tennyson

Dryas
octopetala

Parrot-tulips

May

cabbage

27

26

For lo, the winter is past,

The rain is over & gone;

The flowers appear on the earth;

The time of the singing of

burds is come

Solomon

28

Phlox
G.F.Wilson

Genista Andreana

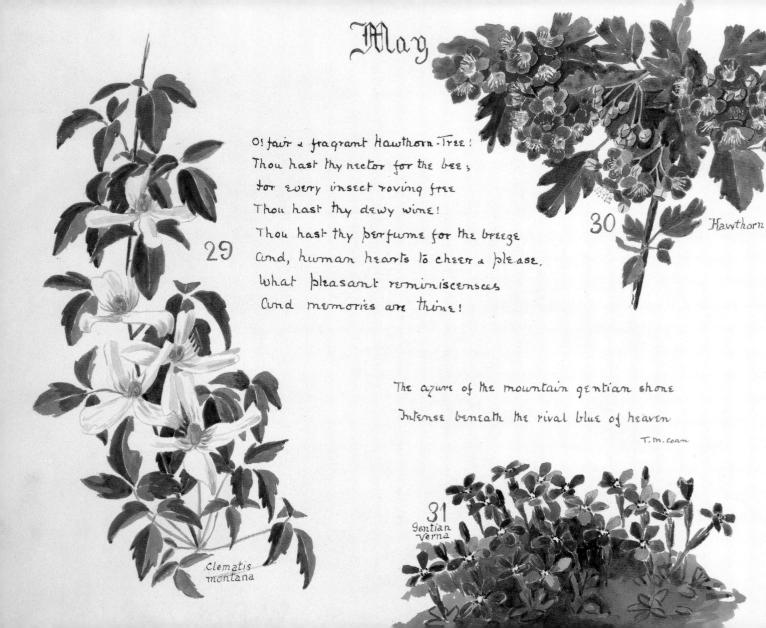

May

O! fair & fragrant Hawthorn-Tree!
Thou hast thy nectar for the bee;
For every insect roving free
Thou hast thy dewy wine!
Thou hast thy perfume for the breeze
And, human hearts to cheer & please,
What pleasant reminiscences
And memories are thine!

29

30   Hawthorn

The azure of the mountain gentian shone
Intense beneath the rival blue of heaven

T. M. Coan

31
Gentian
Verna

Clematis
montana

June

The ways are green with the gladdening sheen
Of the young years fairest daughter.
Laburnum O! the shadows that fleet o'er the
                          springing wheat!
O! the magic of running water!
The spirit of spring is in everything
The banners of spring are streaming
We march to a tune from the fifes of June
And lifes a dream worth dreaming

W. E. Henley

Rubus deliciosus

2

1

Lithospermum coeruleum

3

Welcome, bright June, & all
        its smiling hours,
With song of birds, & stir of leaves
        & wings,
And run of rills, & bubble of
                cool springs,
And hourly burst of pretty
                buds to flowers.

Laburnams dropping wells of fire

Tennyson

C. Webb

Azalea

June

Ramondia
pyrenaica

5

Welcome, sweet stranger, from

the gorgeous East!

4 Nature in thee puts forth her beauteous

might

for aye array'd as for a marriage feast,

Or like an incarnation of pure light.

Coleridge

Pansies

6 Dusky Pansies let them be

for memory

C. Rosetti

7

Viola Rudbergia

June

Roses
Sinica Anemone
Carmine Pillar

8

And the Rose like a nymph
to the bath addrest
Which unveiled the depths of
her glowing breast,
Till fold after fold to the
fainting air
The soul of her beauty
and love lay bare

Shelley

9

Borago Laxiflora

11

Globe-flower

10

Lilac

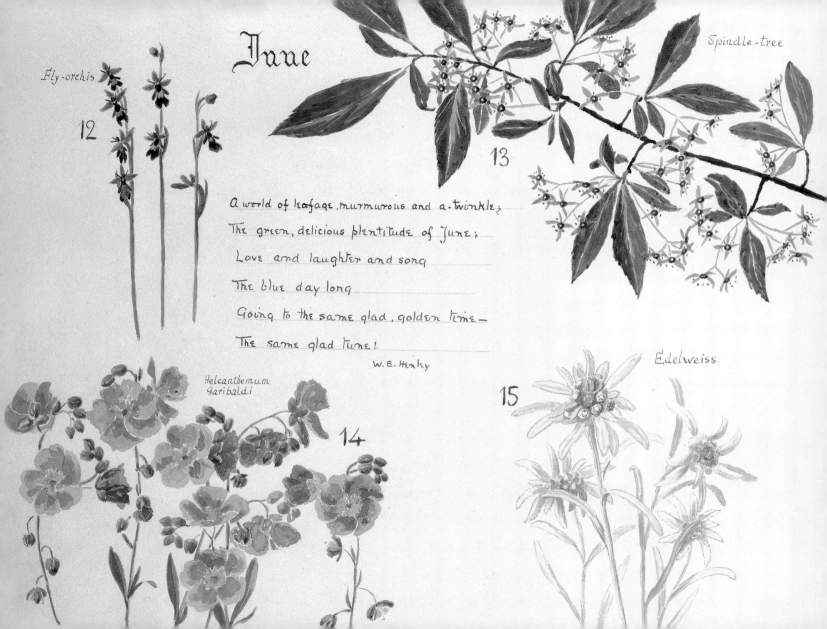

June

Fly-orchis

12

Spindle-tree

13

A world of leafage, murmurous and a-twinkle;

The green, delicious plentitude of June;

Love and laughter and song

The blue day long

Going to the same glad, golden time—

The same glad tune!

W. E. Henley

Helcanthemum
garibaldi

14

Edelweiss.

15

June

Epipactus
(Helleborine)

18

17
Iris
Siberica

Tway-blade

16

The tender delicate flowers,

I saw them fanned by a warm

western wind,

Fed by soft summer showers

A.R. Proctor

June

19

Bladder
Campion

Crowsfoot

20

Deadly Nightshade
(Atropa-Belladonna)

21

.... nightshade's flower of fear

.... Orchis purple & pale

Spotted Palmate
orchis

22

June

Spanish Iris

24

Columbines

The woods green heart is a
nest of dreams,
The lush grass thickens & springs
and sways
The rathe wheat rustles, the
landscape gleams.
Midsummer days!
Midsummer days!

23

25

Wild-rose

A soul from the honeysuckle
strays
And the nightingale as from
prophet heights
Sings to the earth of her million mays.
Midsummer nights!
Midsummer nights!

Henley

26

Iceland poppies

And some do say of poppies

That they be the tears of the moon

June

27

Woody Nightshade

Orange Hawkweed

28

29

Camp. Abietina

Sisyrinchium anceps

30

Day-Lily

July

2   Pyrethrum

1

3

Bee-orchis

4

Sain foin

July

Honeysuckle

How sweetly smells the honeysuckle
In the hush'd night, as if the
world were one
Of utter peace, and love,
and gentleness

Tennyson

Soft sunshine, and the sound
Of old forests echoing round,
And the light and smell divine
Of all flowers that breath and shine—

Shelley

Sax. Cymbalaria

Cypripedium spectabile

July

8

9

The pimpernel thrusts out its bloom
of scarlet, closing up
At every passing shower or cloud,
the treasures of its cup

Pimpernell

Here are Sweet peas, on tiptoe for
a flight:
With wings of gentle flush o'er
delicate white,
And taper fingers, catching at
all things
To bind them all about with
tiny rings

11

Keats

*Onosma
taurica*

10

*Penstemon
heterophyllus*

July

12

Scabiosa Caucasica

13

Upright
St. John's-wort

14

D. Fraxinel

July

17

15

16

Sweet slim harebells,

tenderly hung

Wm. Morris

Camp. pulla
C. Miss Willmott

July

18

'Neath the blue of the sky, in the
green of the corn,
It is there that the regal,
red poppies
are born
Clement Scott.

19

20

On its fair fragile stalk
all lightly swaying,
Trembles the Harebell at each
passing breeze. Camp. Haddiana

Quaking grass

21

I pray to you whom God gives gardens, lend
This happy solace which the flowers bestow;
Where pain oppresses, & where few befriend
To cheer their suffering, & to soothe their woe

July

Bell heather

Camp. Carpatica

22

23

Come down to that old garden
Of every flower we knew,
When out of gates of childhood
The airs of morning blew,
And arching Heaven was painted
In every drop of dew.

Red shall the heather bloom
O'er hill and valley

R.L.S.

24

Cow wheat

25

Erythroea
diffusa

July

The Rose is sweetest washed with morning dew,
27
And Love is loveliest

when embalm'd in tears
Scott

26

The Garden Silence! Even the single bee
Persisting in his toil, suddenly stopt;
And where he hid you only could surmise
By some campanula chalice set a-swing.
Browning

Irish Elegance

Creeping
bell-flower

Penstemon

July

28

29

Camp. Waldsteiniana

July

oxalis
atro-purpurea

30

31

Everlasting pea
Grandiflora

August

Vittadenia or
Erigeron mucronatum

2

1

Convolvulus
althaeoides

3

Corn
Marigold

August

Fuchsia

5

4

Borkhausia
rubra

The gardens, too, in dazzling hues full-blown,

With wafted scent & blazing petals strewn

R. Bridges

6

Con. mauritanicus

August

7

Yellow-Melilot

8

g-asphodel

Raspberry

9

Mountain everlastin

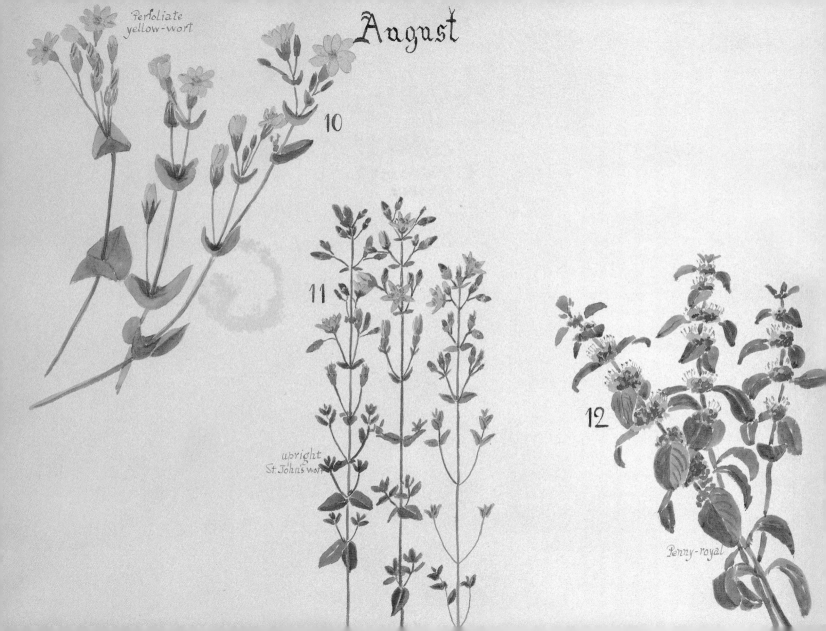

Perfoliate
yellow-wort

August

10

11

upright
St John's wort

12

Penny-royal

August

Astilbe Davidii

13

Romneya Coulteri

14

August

15

Eryngium
amethystinum

16

Zauschneria

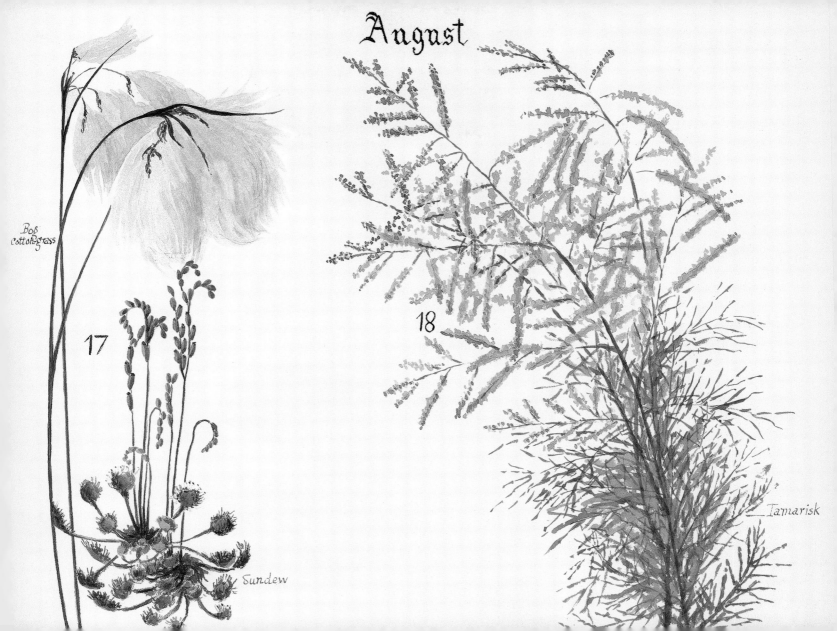

August

Bog
Cotton-grass

17

Sundew

18

Tamarisk

August

19
Snow-berry

20

Diascoea
Barbarae

21

Calycanthus
occidentalis

August

23

Myrtle

22

24

Balloon-flower

Eomecon
chionantha

August

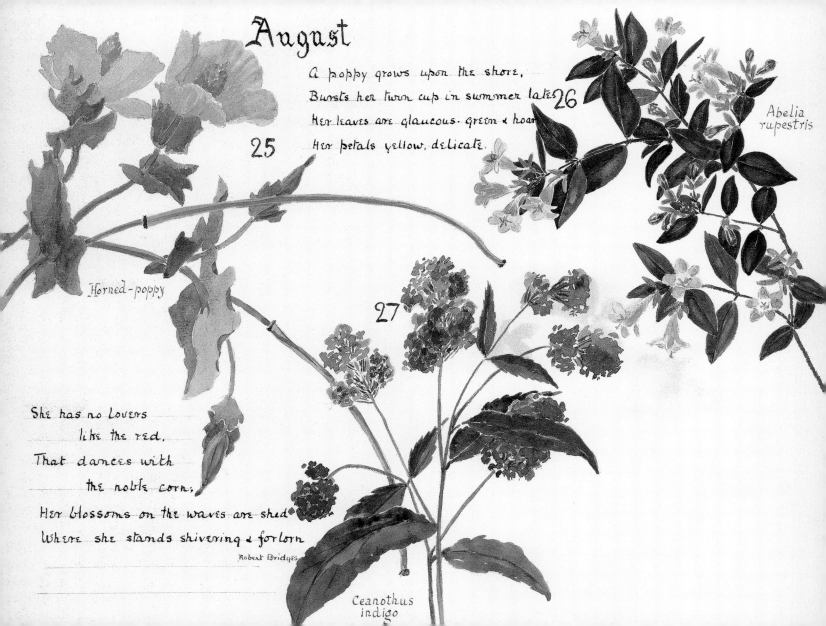

A poppy grows upon the shore,
Bursts her twin cup in summer late
Her leaves are glaucous, green & hoar
Her petals yellow, delicate.

25

26

Abelia
rupestris

Horned-poppy

27

She has no lovers
        like the red,
That dances with
        the noble corn;
Her blossoms on the waves are shed
Where she stands shivering & forlorn

Robert Bridges

Ceanothus
indigo

28

Chrysogonum
virginicum

Tropæolum
speciosum

29

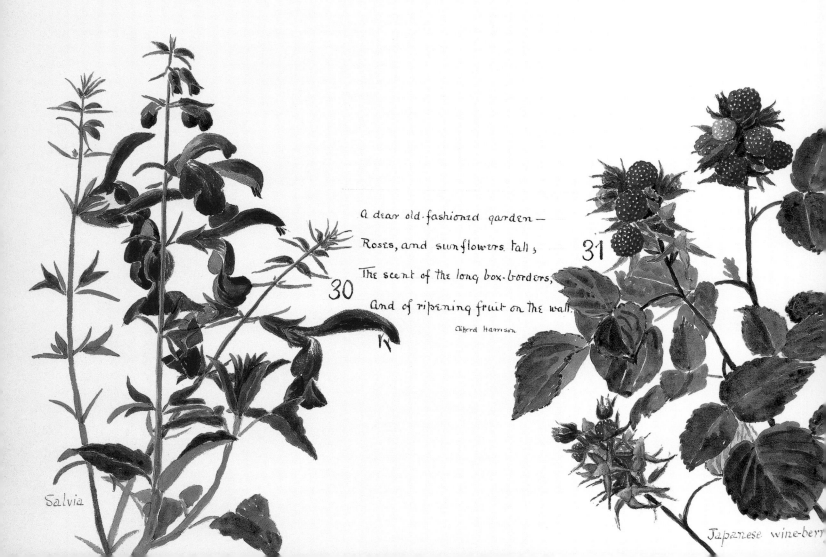

A dear old-fashioned garden —
Roses, and sunflowers, tall;
The scent of the long box-borders,
And of ripening fruit on the wall.

Clifford Harrison

30

31

Salvia

Japanese wine-berry

September

Buddleia

1

Clematis Jackmani

2

September

Grass of
Parnassus

3

Those peerless flowers which in the rudest wind

Never grow sere

Tennyson

Clematis Jackmani

4

Anemone
japonica

5

September

Through the dancing poppies stole
A breeze most softly lulling to my soul;
And shaping visions all about my sight
Of colours, winds, & bursts of spangly light!

Keats

6
Aster (annual)

7
Hypericum
Moserianum

8
Shirley
Poppies

September

If I could paint you the Autumn colour, the melting gold
upon all things laid,

The violet haze of Indian summer, before its splendour
begins to fade,

When scarlet has reached its breathless moment, & gold
the hush of its glory now,

That were a mightier craft than

Titian's, the heart to lift & the head to bow

Bliss Carmen

Helenium

9

Nasturtium

10

11

Aster Linosyris

September

Scabious (annual)

12

13

Colchicum
speciosum

14

Hardy Cyclamen

September

Lemon Calceolaria

15

Bergamot

16

17

Erigeron philadelphu

Devil's-bit scabious

September

18

19

Tradescantia
virginica

20

Knapweed

September

Giant cone-flower

21

22

Briony

Autumn evening, and the morn,
when the golden mists are born.
Shelley

Polygonum
vaccinifolium

23

24

Irish-heath

September

Sloe berries

25

26

27

Autumn beareth fruit whilst day by day
The leaves grow browner with a
mellow hue,
Declining to a beautiful decay

C. Rossetti

Japanese
anemone

Silver-weed

September

Rudbeckia

29

28

Single Dahlias

30

Alpine thistle

Cotoneaster
rupestris

1

Chrysanthemum
uliginosum

2

Frost nips the weak, while strengthening

still the strong

Against that day when Spring sets all to rights

C. Rossetti

Toad-stools

3

Chrysanthemum
uliginosum

October

Virginia creeper

The Sunflower weary of time
Who countest the steps of the sun
Seeking after that sweet golden clime
Where the travellers journey is done.

Blake

Toad-stools

5

6

Helianthu

Helia

Hawthorn - haws

October

7

Rosa · Rugosa · hips

8

The thorns & briars, vermilion hue,
how full of hips & haws are seen,
If village-prophecies be true
They prove that winter will be keen.

He that high growth of cedars
          did bestow,
Gave also lowly mushrooms   Mushrooms
          leave to grow
                    R. Southwell

9

October

Aster Thompsoni

out-door chrysanthemum

10

11

12

The wind-flower & the violet, they perished long ago,
And the brier-rose & the orchis died amid the summer glow
But on the hill the goldenrod, & the aster in the wood,
And the yellow sun-flower by the brook, in autumn beauty stood
Till fell the frost from the clear cold heaven, as falls the
                                    plague on men,
And the brightness of their smile was gone from upland, glade & glen

W. C. Bryant

October

Centaurea
Ruthenica

Elder-berries

The woods shall wear their robes
of praise
The south wind gently sigh
And sweet calm days in golden haze
melt in the amber sky.

Whittier

14

13

O! sound to rout the brood of cares,
The sweep of scythe in morning dew,
The gust that round the garden flew,
And tumbled half the mellowing pears

Tennyson

16

15

Lavender

Pear _ Durondeau

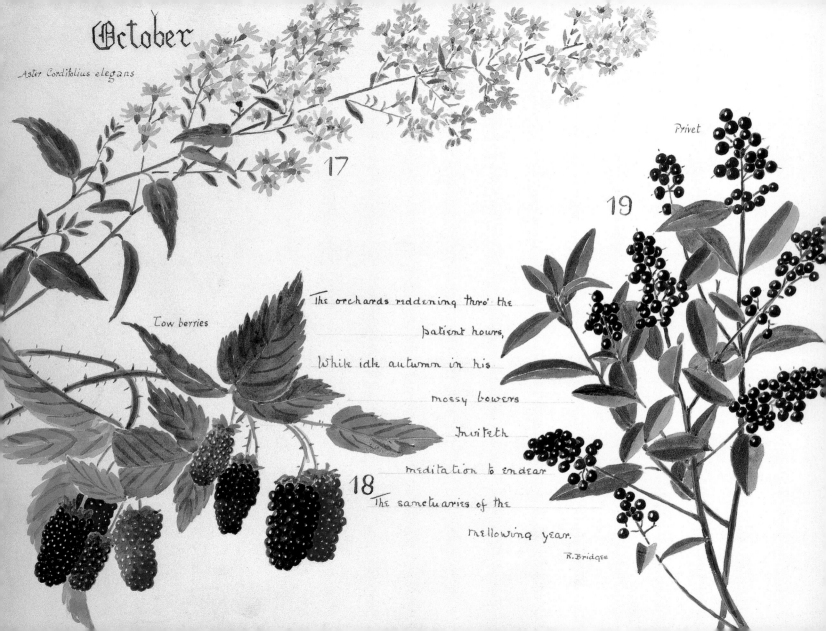

October

Aster Cordifolius elegans

17

Privet

19

Low berries

The orchards reddening thro' the
patient hours,
While idle autumn in his
mossy bowers
Inviteth
meditation to endear
The sanctuaries of the
mellowing year.

18

R. Bridges

October

Wayfaring Tree, what ancient claim
Hast thou to that right pleasant name?
Was it that some faint pilgrim came
Unhopedly to thee,
In the brown desert's weary way,
And there, as 'neath thy
shade he lay,
'mid toil and thirst's consuming
sway
Bless'd the Wayfaring Tree?

Horse-chestnut

20

On frosty morns
with the woods aflame, down down
The golden spoils fall thick
from the chestnut
crown
R. Bridges

Seeds of Mealy-Guelder-rose
(Wayfaring Tree)

21

The time of the silence
Of birds is upon us;
Rust in the chestnut leaf,
Dust in the stubble:
The turn of the Year
And the call to decay
W. E. Henley

Seeds of Lords & Ladies

22

Turkish Oak

October

Aster pulchellus

And thanks for the harvest
of beauty,
for that which the hands
cannot hold,
The harvest eyes only can gather
And only our hearts can enfold.

23

24

Aster rosea

25

26

Growths on
Wild rose

27

Geum
Bradshaw

Heliotrope

28

29

Salvia

October

Heuchera Edge-Hall

30

Spring, the young morn, & Summer, the strong noon

Have dreamed & done & died for Autumn's sake

R. le Gallienne

Ageratum

31

..... like the garden, where the year is spent,

The ruin of old life is full of yearning,

Mingling poetic rapture of lament

With flowers & sunshine of spring's sure returning

R. Bridges

November

Cosmos

1

Mullein

3

2

Plantain

Summer is gone with all
its roses,
Its sun & perfume & sweet
flowers,
Its warm air and refreshing showers:
And even Autumn closes.
Yea, Autumn's chilly self is going,
And Winter comes which is yet
colder;
Each day the hoar frost waxes
bolder
And the last
buds
cease blowing

C. Rossetti

November

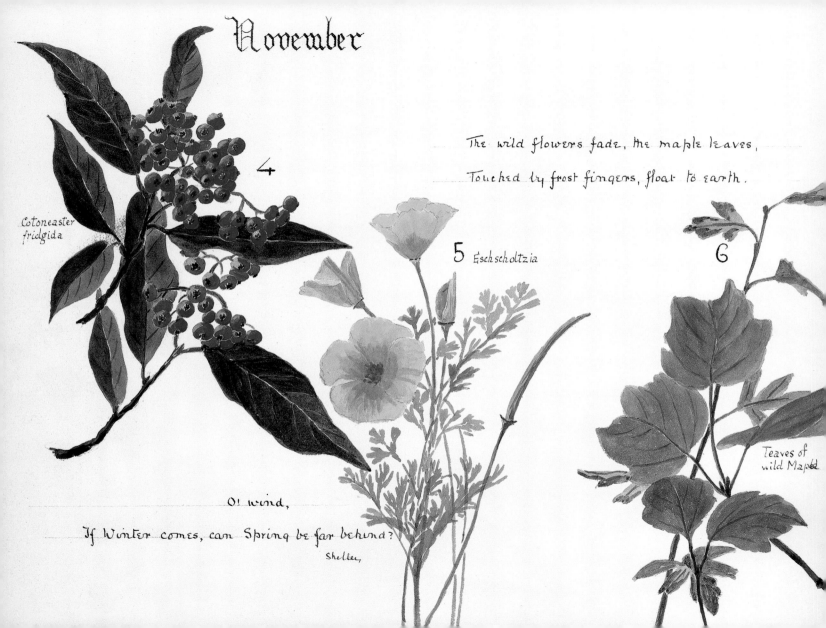

The wild flowers fade, the maple leaves,

Touched by frost fingers, float to earth.

Cotoneaster
fridgida

4

5 Eschscholtzia

6

Teaves of
wild Maple

O! wind,

If Winter comes, can Spring be far behind?

Shelley.

Mustard

Asparagus

7

8

Catkins of
Hazel

9

November

Thou shouldst bloom surely in some
sunny clime.

Untouched by blights and chilly
winters rime

C. Rossetti

Hips of wild
white-rose

10

Berries of
woody nightshade

Late blooming rose

Frau K. D.

11

12

The splendours of the summer time
are done,

And though the roses linger for a space,

Soon they will fade on paths and
garden ways.

The russet leaves lie thickly, and the sun

Wakes late now, and his course is
swiftly run.

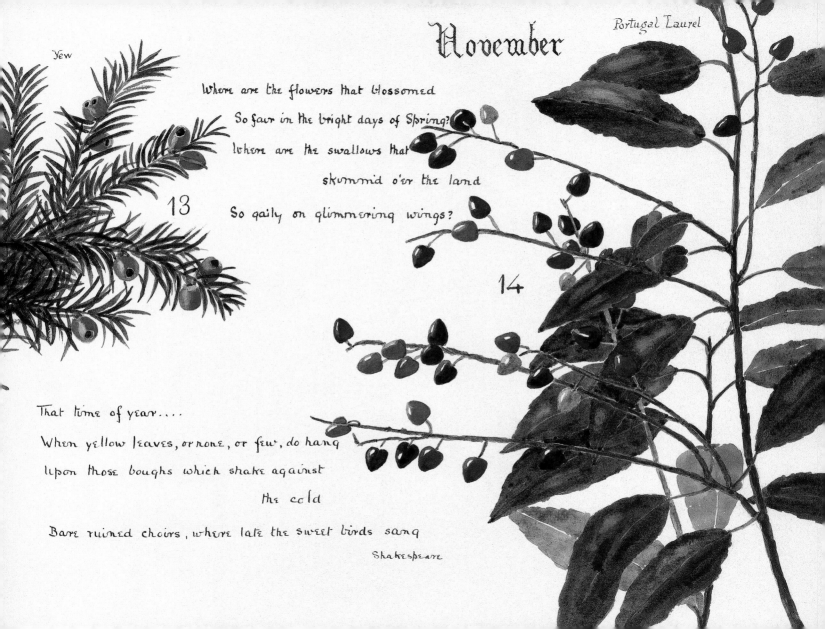

November

Where are the flowers that blossomed
So fair in the bright days of Spring?
Where are the swallows that
skimmed o'er the land
So gaily on glimmering wings?

13

14

That time of year....
When yellow leaves, or none, or few, do hang
Upon those boughs which shake against
the cold
Bare ruined choirs, where late the sweet birds sang

Shakespeare

November

Aster horizontalis

Sow-thistle

Alpine
toad-flax

15
The garden ground is sown with grief.

. . . .

There is no comfort in the year,

Despair has slowly tolled his knell;

The world's existence is a fear,

And life but one supreme farewell.

But O: my love! remember this:

There must be birth & blossoming;

Nature will waken with a kiss

Next Spring!

Clement Scott

17

16

November

Spindle-tree

20

Those few Autumn Flowers,
  How beautiful they are!
Than all that went before
Than all the summer store.
  How lovelier far!

19

18

Escallonia

Phygelius capensis

Pale flowers! pale perishing flowers!
  Ye're types of precious things;
Types of those little moments
That flit like life's enjoyments
  On rapid, rapid wings.

C. Southey

November 21 Winter cherry

Gazania 22

23 Acaena advergens

November

Ampelopsis Veitchii

24

Camomile

25

Self-heal

26

27

Cuphea strigulosa

But you are lovely leaves, where we

may read how soon things have

Their end, though ne'er so brave

And after they have shown

their pride

Like you, awhile, they glide

Into the grave

Herrick

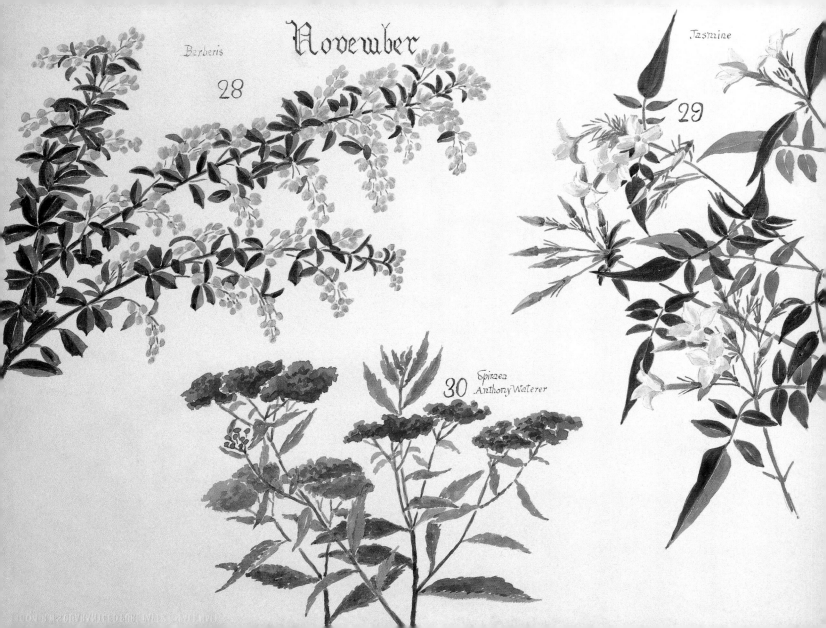

November

Berberis

28

Jasmine

29

30 Spiræa
Anthony Waterer

December

Faint scented, pinched upon its stalk
The least and last which cold winds balk,
A Rose it is, though least & last of all
A Rose to me though at the fall

C. Rossetti

Spiraea acuta

1

2

'Tis the Last Rose of Summer left blooming alone
All its lovely companions are faded & gone

T. Moore

3

Seeds of Veronica
Traversii

Last rose
of Summer

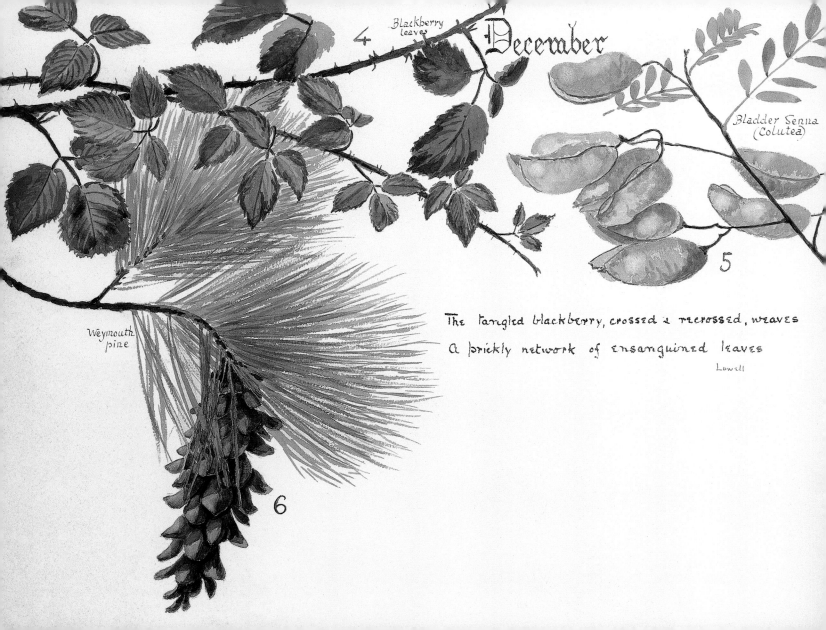

Blackberry
leaves

4

December

Bladder Senna
(Colutea)

5

Weymouth
pine

6

The tangled blackberry, crossed & recrossed, weaves
A prickly network of ensanguined leaves

Lowell

December

The sun's away,
And the bird estranged;
The wind has dropped
And the sky's deranged:
Summer hasstopped

Browning

C.Pyracantha

Seeds of
Hemlock

7

8

Douglas pine

9

December

Arbutus

10

11

Seeds of Broom

12

Late
chrysanthemu

Azalea

December

13

Outside the garden the wet skies harden;
the gates are barred on
The Summer side

Swinburne

14

Summer is gone on swallow's wings,
And Earth has buried all her flowers.....
Farewell...... but thou wilt come again
On the gay wings of butterflies.....
Roses shall be where roses were,
Not shadows, but reality

Tom Hood

Seeds of
Jasmine

December

Crab-apple

15

16

Veron

December

17

Gerbera
Jamesoni

18

Seeds of Figwort

19

Erigeron
acris

Thy garden of pleasure

Lies withered and bare,

O! the pitiless measure

Of ruin wrought there!

M. Bell

Let us once go dreaming down the old

old way,

Though the mantle of December hide the

face of May;

Something of the old songs with us

will remain,

While we weave the gray world into green again.

W. Akerman

Coral Barberry

December

20

21

Carline thistle

Plumbago Larpentae

22

'Tis a dull sight

To see the year dying

When winter winds

Set the yellow woods sighing:

Sighing, O sighing

E. Fitzgerald

December

23

Honesty

24

Laurestinus

December

25

Holly

26

Mistletoe

December

Pernettya 27

Pernetty.

28

29

Winter
Heliotrope

Skimmia
japonica

31 *Golden-holly*

30

Solanum